SACRED SYMBOLS
OF
BUDDHISM

J.R. SANTIAGO

BOOK FAITH INDIA
Delhi

SACRED SYMBOLS OF BUDDHISM

J.R.Santiago

Published by

BOOK FAITH INDIA
(An imprint of)
PILGRIMS BOOK HOUSE (NEW DELHI)
1626, Raj Guru Road, Chuna mandi,
pahar Ganj, New Delhi 110055
Tel: 91-11-23584015
Fax: 91-11-23584019
E-mail: pilgrim@del2.vsnl.net.in
E-mail: pilgrimsinde@gmail.com

Artwork and text design by Dr. Sasya
Layout by Naresh Subba

1st Edition
Copyright © 1999 Book Faith India

ISBN 81-7303-182-7

Printed in India

CONTENTS

Preface

This is a brief survey of the sacred symbols of Buddhism. The evolution and development of Buddhism flowed from the vast spiritual landscape of India. Its form and concepts slowly evolved from the sacred symbols of Hinduism, nurtured in its growth, like a lotus in the matrix of India.

The Buddhist sacred symbols and attributes have not diverged completely, in connotation or meaning, from their counterparts in Hinduism. There is only a slight variation in purpose, but when perceived they reveal their origin in the great past of the Hindu creed.

Like the Hindu sacred symbols, the Buddhist symbols remain unique and fascinating in their exotic form and esoteric significance. They provide a deeper insight into the religious phenomena of the subcontinent, the Himalayas and Tibet, the mysterious land on the roof of the world.

Like any other spiritual symbols, they do not merely explain or resolve seemingly contradictory spiritual concepts, but instruct on the way of attaining enlightenment.

FOREWORD

O ut of the broad sweep of the spiritual landscape of Hinduism emerged Buddhism, an entirely new creed, not concerned with the question of the existence of God, but with salvation from the misery of human earthly experience.

It blazed a completely new path, with a new goal attainable by new but practical means. Although completely at variance with its matrix of evolution — Hinduism — it was only natural that it borrowed sacred symbols and ritual artefacts. Other paraphernalia of worship, along with the Hindu deities and their attributes, were assimilated mainly because they had already become institutionalized, were traditional and deeply rooted in the cultural psyche of the land.

Everything, except for the philosophy, but not the metaphysical basis, was taken up and assimilated into the new religious ideology. This remained unaltered for a long time, retaining the original names, purpose and significance. Small changes occurred but with only slight variations in significance and meaning. In the course of time new paraphernalia began to appear; they were different, but they remained in concept analogous to the central original religious cultural paraphernalia of Hinduism.

The esoteric symbols of Buddhism therefore remain shrouded with the essence of the ancient prehistoric creed: the aura, which evokes the mystical aspects bestowed on them from the very beginning of their evolution.

Without a background in Hinduism they spring up as not merely exoteric but esoteric, they are numerous and pervasive: they are almost everywhere, in temples, houses, shops, the streets, the forests, hills, rocks and river banks. Most of them are covered with a patina of age, coming as they do from the primal mists of time, and are therefore mostly unintelligible.

The purpose of this introductory book on the sacred symbols of Buddhism is to explain their meaning and significance in a nutshell, to try to make them comprehensible. To make it easier to understand the evolution of a new creed — a new human experience. Like a bud evolving and blossoming into a flower, which began to waft its scent around the world two thousand years ago.

Introduction

The primary inspiration in the evolution of Buddhism was the discovery of human suffering caused by diseases, poverty and old age, ending in death. This is the inevitable consequence of life from birth, recognized and treated by Hinduism, but mainly concerned with the Underlying Principle of human existence and of the phenomenal universe.

Buddhism deals primarily and directly with the reality of human existence by delving into the mind and human consciousness. It is not concerned with or seeks to deny the metaphysical fundamentals of life and the cosmos. It emphasizes the alleviation of the human condition, based on human psychology, employing analytical methods and finally taking up meditation, the spiritual path that led Siddhartha into Buddhahood.

The human being is a composite of body, mind and spirit. It focuses on the mind and its psychological insight is indeed incisive and profound, for its constitution affects the body and the spirit. It is really holistic in its approach. For enlightenment, which brings salvation, the Buddha laid out The Four Noble Truths and The Eightfold Paths. The Four Noble Truths are constructed on the logic of syllogism with the proposition or premise — the thesis:—

1. That suffering is caused by worldly bonds;
2. That its origin is linked to *samsara*, the cycle of human existence, caused by desire, such as lust, possession and happiness;
3. That suffering must be eliminated by the destruction of desire through the elimination of ignorance;

4.   And that the elimination of ignorance, the ultimate cause of human misery, must be made through The Eightfold Paths which leads to enlightenment.

The Eightfold Paths recommend the following:-

1.   Right understanding.
2.   Right attitude,
3.   Right speech,
4.   Right action,
5.   Right conduct,
6.   Right effort,
7.   Right attention or mindfulness,
8.   Right meditation

These are the dynamics, the mechanism and the process of attaining enlightenment and therefore salvation. This involves seeking sanctuary in The Three Jewels, made up of The Buddha, the embodiment of enlightenment; the Dharma, the Cosmic Law; and The Sangha, the community of monks. Everyone therefore has to become a student, a disciple or a monk for his education, training and enlightenment.

Conscious of karmic differences in human evolution the Buddha propounded the Three Vehicles representing three levels: the school, college or university and the postgraduate:

1.   Hinayana — The Small Vehicle
        Also known as Theravada, its basic doctrine is that enlightenment can be achieved alone, by self-discipline, by studying The Four Noble Truths and following The Eightfold Paths. The aim is to reach Nirvana, a state of peace, the final emancipation. This method could cover many lifetimes before Nirvana could be attained.

2.   Mahayana — The Large Vehicle
        Known as the Middle Doctrine — The Middle Path — it teaches moderation. This requires the assistance of an enlightened teacher. It leads to Buddhahood, but its main precept is the enlightenment of everybody. Hence, the teacher defers Buddhahood until everybody has been enlightened. The

goal is the Absolute Void.

3.   Vajrayana — The Diamond Vehicle
        Known as Tantrayana, its doctrine is that everyone is a potential
Buddha, and that enlightenment can be attained in a single lifetime. Every
element in human nature, considered as energy, is utilized in the attainment of
enlightenment. This is considered the highest, but is extremely difficult.

        This introductory work on Mahayana symbolism deals on the whole
with Tantrayana mystical concepts. Being pre-Vedic, it was pervasive all over
the subcontinent including the Himalaya and Tibet, where, isolated for centuries
from the outside world, it retained the original and pure form of occult practices.

        In particular the Tibetans developed many of their own symbols,
which are original in concept. Along with the emergence of different deities,
there developed also different divine attributes, ritual artefacts and
paraphernalia in ritual worship. They naturally acquired a different
significance from those of Hinduism and to a slight extent, from those of the
Mahayana discipline.

        With the Tibetan exodus in the early 1960s when China occupied
Tibet, the influx of Tibetans into the subcontinent brought about the introduction
and spread of the sacred symbols. In a modern world these symbols seem
strange, mysterious, and steeped in occult science or mysticism.

        Because of its syncretistic nature, a background knowledge of
Hinduism would help the reader to understand Vajrayana and the Mahayana
symbolism to a greater extent by association. Also by extension the symbolism
of pre-Vedic creeds, the original source of their evolution.

BUDDHISM

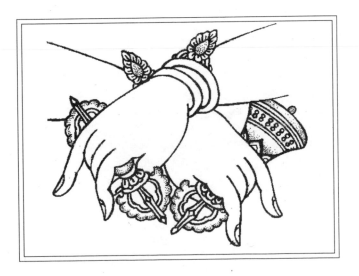

Compassion is the essence of Buddhism. In Tibetan this is known as Nin-jhi. It is compassion towards all living creatures, but most of all towards oneself. One must liberate oneself from human suffering, which will eventually culminate in a spiritual quest.

Worship is not central to the teachings of the Buddha, but in the development of Buddhism the Buddha himself is now worshipped. It is more a form of emulation of an exemplary human being who became a Buddha. It is because of him that a monk or student is aware that he himself is a potential Buddha.

Along with the old Hindu deities, there is now a proliferation of Bodhisattvas who are worshipped; but worship is not the Dharma — The Law. The Dharma must be studied and followed, or even worshipped.

The Law is practical, direct and incisive. It delves into the human psyche, the basic source of suffering. It contains the philosophy, the principles and the symbols to help acquire a deeper insight into human nature, which teaches that perfection is attainable.

In the Third Vehicle — Vajrayana, or the Diamond Vehicle, Buddhism and Hinduism tread on the same pre-Vedic mystical practice of Tantrism. In the end the would-be Bodhisattva must go it alone.

It is a lonely struggle. The Buddha has a powerful influence on the human mind, for his solitary figure evokes and exudes from the deepest source — the Absolute Void — the profound unfathomable quietude of a quiescent being who has attained perfection. Alone, the monk, or aspirant dwells on his own being, relying mainly on himself to attain perfection.

His ultimate and mystical destiny is back to the Source from whence he came — The Void.

Symbols as Sacred Art

Emerging out of the deeply mystical spiritual landscape of India, Buddhism naturally absorbed, almost by osmosis, the philosophy and principles already institutionalized as traditions in the culture of Hinduism. And Tantra in particular was pervasive, it was not adopted, but was inherent in the mystical lore of the land.

Thus Buddhist Tantrayana has the same basic philosophy, principles, ritual artefacts and symbols as Tantrism in Hinduism.

Tantric art has for its purpose the attainment of a higher level of perception. Its real significance lies, not in its aesthetic value, but in the philosophy of life it displays. 'Tantra art is visual metaphysics'. It is a synthesis of the external and internal worlds. The psychophysical unity, man's link with the cosmos, is a reality.

They are allegorical, products of creative psychic manifestations. Their real significance lies in their enigmatic metaphysical undertones. It is in this symbolism that the real is made visible; it becomes a visual aid for self-enlightenment.

The symbols are ageless, they have survived ages, through generations. They have a timeless quality representing governing principles of life. Tantric art has for its goal emancipation from ignorance: it is to realize what is intuitively known. This is the motif of the entire symbolism.

The symbols are interrelated and form the whole concept of a mystical doctrine, which leads in the end to the struggle to find its basic element in the human heart – the spirit – the Divine Spark.

The physical world is the workshop in which to realize the inner reality for a deep sense of fulfillment – enlightenment.

Vajrayana

The Four Noble Truths and the Eightfold Paths, the Hinayana and the Mahayana Vehicles are original and exclusive Buddhist concepts. The Vajrayana or Tantrayana Vehicle was adopted as Buddhist training, eventually culminated in a spiritual quest.

Vajrayana, the thunderbolt path, also known as the Diamond Vehicle, is the most powerful of all the three Buddhist vehicles.

Mahayana, the Large Vehicle, also known as the Middle Doctrine, identifies the overall Buddhist creed in the subcontinent, in the Himalayas and Tibet. It is fundamentally in agreement with Vajrayana, in that everyone is a potential Buddha. It requires the assistance of an enlightened guru to attain enlightenment.

In Mahayana, however, Buddhahood is a group endeavour, with the attainment of the Absolute Void deferred even over several lifetimes until everyone is ready. In Tantra, because of its power-method and individual struggle, Buddhahood could be achieved in an amazingly quick manner, not over several lifetimes but in a single lifetime.

Vajrayana, in its mystical secrecy, appears subsumed under Mahayana, but it is the real spirit, the substance, the light that illuminates Buddhism. Its occult art or sciences evoke mysticism. Its central method is yogic meditation, which is considered supreme.

It is apparently in principle, but not metaphysically, antithetical with the core teaching of the Buddha in regard to human desire — the cause of human misery — for it is this very weakness that is employed in tantra. The desire, the intense passion, is harnessed and used in the attainment of Buddhahood. Its fundamental characteristics remain; detachment, asceticism, and renunciation of worldly life.

It is the same Tantra that emerges supreme in the attainment of self-realization in Hinduism. It is for the same reason therefore that, except for the Tibetan variations, Buddhist symbols remain practically the same as Hindu. Central to the system are also the three principles called the *Triguya:* the yantra for the spirit, the mantras for the mind or soul, and the asanas or physical yogic exercises for the body.

Vajrayana expounds a mystical philosophy and applies the three principles of action all together in a concentrated powerful way to attain Buddhahood.

In Tibetan Vajrayana there are three major symbols: the bell, the vajra or dorje, and the thunderbolt scepter. Together they represent incorruptible purity of the diamond — the truth — that no force can destroy.

II

MYSTICAL SYMBOLS

Like the Vajrayana Vehicle the mystical symbols have been adopted from Hinduism, almost practically unaltered, except for a slight variation to suit the new creed.

MANDALA

This is a pre-Vedic religious device that was already in use in Tantric rituals. It was adopted by followers of the Vajrayana discipline.

In its configuration it is a circle. A circle has a universal mystical protective significance. In the Ramayana epic, Lakshman, the brother of Rama made a circle around Sita, his sister-in-law before leaving her alone, for protection in the jungle.

In Mahayana Buddhism, 'Manda' means 'what is contained, defended or held' and 'la' means that 'which contains, defends or holds'. Thus it is a circle which holds and defends what it contains. In the Buddhist mystical doctrine it is the deity consecrated in the mandala.

It is generally a symbolic graphic design, a visual aid in Tantric meditation, for the purpose of attaining insight and activating supernatural forces latent in the human body.

The best or special mandala is prepared by an enlightened teacher for his disciple and is not sold or bartered but is given. In its preparation, before work can start, the guru must undergo fasting and meditate on its design and the particular mantra appropriate to it. He must remain in isolation for a period of time for purification, for it is a sacred act.

The design can be prepared on the ground, a rock, metal or crystal, but generally on wood or paper. The best material is crystal rock, for it is clean, colorless, and transparent, which can be shaped so as to focus light at the apex. It is a substance that has all other substances for its elements.

It begins simply as a dot. A line is drawn; other lines are made extending in specified directions until they intersect and create geometrical triangular patterns. A circle is drawn around them, which then becomes enclosed in a square.

The upright triangles stand for the masculine principle; the inverted triangles for the feminine principle. The circle represents the dynamic consciousness of the creator; the outlying squares the physical world bound in four directions; and the lotus petals around the circle represent the regenerative power and principle. The center is the residence of the deity.

The creative process is a gathering of external surrounding forces, in the act of drawing, the creator's own energy unfolds and is gathered simultaneously. The purpose is to remove the subject-object dichotomy. When this is completed, it is then consecrated to a particular deity by chanting the appropriate mantra and inscribing the appropriate Sanskrit syllables in the mandala to transform it into energy-power house representing the deity.

The diagrammatic design becomes a yantra, a symbol of worship.

The center piece of a mandala could be an icon, aniconic objects or symbolic artefacts like the lingam, the trident of Shiva, or the discus of Vishnu, but they have to be consecrated in the ritual diagrammatic design for the mandala to become a yantra.

In Tantric Buddhism the mandala represents the 'Palace of Purity,' where all obstacles and impurities are removed. The square stands for the 'Sacred Palace', which is surrounded by a circle of flames, four thunderbolts, eight cemeteries, and a lotus. The inner square is the center where the deity is propitiated.

YANTRA

In Buddhism a sacred mandala is a yantra. It represents what is visible and knowable: the concentrated energy in the mandala.

The term has two aspects: 'Yan' means to regulate' and 'tra' means to protect. It is therefore an instrument in which the psychophysical energies of the worshipper are regulated and protected. Thus regulation is protection.

Among the Buddhist Tantrics, the preparation of a yantra is practically analogous to the process followed by the Hindu Tantrics. It must be prepared by an enlightened teacher, who must meditate on the design of the mandala, which must also not be sold or bartered, but given to a disciple.

It is therefore similarly a sacred undertaking. The only difference is that the Buddhist deities, some of whom have been adopted from Hinduism, are consecrated in the mandala. The object and effect of worship is also similar. In worship the consciousness of the devotee finds expression. In its articulation it is expanded beyond subjective feelings and the external forces around, and in their interaction evolves spiritual development.

In Tibetan Buddhism a yantra is called Qing-quo and is of many kinds for a variety of deities and purposes. In Tibetan Surya Puja — Greetings to the Rising Sun — the mandala is adorned with flowers, saffron water, incense, and a representation of Mt. Sumeru, the mythical seat of the deity, said to be the center of the universe.

Sri Yantra

In the Vajrayana discipline Sri Yantra is also known in Tibetan as Kalachakra and considered the supreme mystical mandala. It represents the inner and outer world — the unity of both the microcosm and the macrocosm.

The meaning and significance of symbols in the yantra remain the same as in the original context practised by the Hindu Tantrics: the equilateral intersecting triangles also represent the union of the female and male principles. Their inseparability is the most important significance.

Except in the representation of spaces in the mandala, the Buddhist and Hindu Sri Yantras are analogous, for involved is Kamakala, its fundamental principle.

'Kama' means desire; 'ka' means emanation; and 'la' means the end or absorption. It is represented by a triangle. In its original form it is made of a dot above two other dots below. The dot above represents kama; the two dots below stand for ka emanation and la for withdrawal. From kama the line stands for desire (first principle), moves towards the dot below which stands for emanation (second principle), which continues towards the dot which stands for withdrawal (third principle).

KALACHAKRA

Among the Hindus this is known as the Sri Chakra. In Buddhism this is known as the Wheel of Time, usually illustrated in a thangka or sacred Tibetan painting, which is regarded as activating the internal as well as the external forces, like a yantra. It is actually constructed like a stupa, with a square base followed by a mandala, and in the middle is the pinnacle, a representation of Mt. Sumeru, the residence of a deity. It represents the possibility of attaining enlightenment in a single lifetime.

The Wheel of Life is another Tibetan ritual painting like a yantra. It symbolizes the supreme aim of life — enlightenment.

In Tibetan the kalachakra puja is called Dam-jho which is particularly important during this time of great difficulties — of wars and natural disasters. The kalachakra is called the mandala of four doors or Qing-ghou.

The kalachakra apparently is the favorite of His Holiness, the Dalai Lama, as a ritual worship. The reason is that it is very powerful in activating spiritual development. Only the Dalai Lama is believed to be able to perform it many times. It is reportedly so powerful that ordinary lamas can only do it three times. Beyond three they apparently die.

Again it is only the lamas or the Dalai Lama who can perform the kalachakra. When the ritual is over, the mandala is destroyed, and usually thrown into a lake or river.

OM

This is the most sacred mantra, which is regarded as the primal sound in the birth of the cosmos.

Its symbol is OM, but the actual mystic sound heard in the deep meditative state is A-U-M, which appears to correspond to the three elements __that sprang up out of creation: Spirit-mind-body. 'A' stands for the initial surge of emanation; 'U' for preserving or nurturing it; and 'M' for absorption, not dissolution. It also stands for Brahma-Vishnu-Shiva, the Hindu trinity.

When articulated or chanted, it is cleansing or purifying, and activates certain latent forces in the human body, and helps transcends worldly problems. Hence, as the holiest of all mantras, it must precede all other mantras, otherwise the latter would not have the presence of divine power or force. To make any work successful, it must be invoked before the work is started.

It is regarded to exist before and after creation. It is imperishable and therefore the symbol of the Infinite. It resides and is present in Silence, and represents the entire manifested and unmanifested world.

Mantra

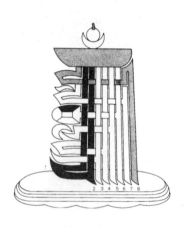

Mantras are power-words - prayers - either articulated loudly with proper sound and rhythm, or chanted.

'Man' means the mind and 'tra' means to guide or protect. It is thus the protector of the mind. It signifies a sacred reality, and is chanted in ritual worship to invest it with the grace of a deity.

It is dynamic, like the breath of life, it endows a ritual artefact with the essence of what is sacred. As an aid in meditation, it apparently awakens latent spiritual forces in the human body.

Like everything else it is the intention - the motivating spirit - that gives significance to a word or name and makes it a power-word.

Om Mane Padme Hum

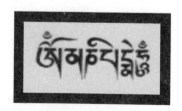

This is a Tibetan mantra. It means 'Hail! To The Jewel In The Lotus'. It refers to conscious knowledge of the existence of the jewel — the Divine Spark — in the human heart.

TRIANGLE

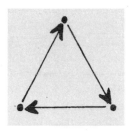

The triangle, the male principle, represents the unmanifested power of resurgence.

INVERTED TRIANGLE

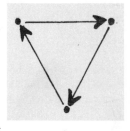

The inverted triangle stands for the female principle — the yoni. It has two dots above with one dot below all linked up by lines.

This appears more the proper symbol for creation: From the dot below, which stands for kama, springs up desire. A line descending towards the dot for emanation continues horizontally towards the dot representing withdrawal, and from here descends downward back to the dot below — the source.

The cyclical movement of the lines back to the original dot at the bottom represents the power of resurgence inherent in its nature.

CHAKRAS

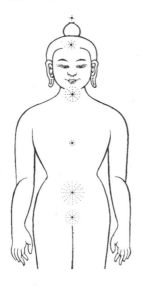

The five chakras representing the five elements in nature, are located in the spinal column. They belong to the subtle body and are not visible. They are contact points for the psychic and the physical body. They are considered centers of energy.

Two other chakras are located in the head: the Ajna chakra — Third Eye — is the center of consciousness; and the Sahasrara chakra, located on top of the head, is the center of pure consciousness or the mind.

KUNDALINI

This is known as the Serpent Power, another name for Shakti, the female energy. When it is asleep, it is coiled three and a half times with its tail in its mouth, at the bottom of the spinal column. When awakened, it hisses with a sibilant sound like a snake as it rises up until it joins the male principle in the Sahasrara chakra.

Yogic Asanas

The asanas are physical exercises of stretching and limbering to make the body flexible, supple and youthful. They involve breathing — pranayama — ending in poses as khumbaka.

The main purpose is to maintain a healthy constitution. However, there are yogic poses or postures combined with pranayama, which are intended to awaken latent forces in the body, particularly the kundalini, the female energy. The intention is to make it rise up the chakras or centers of energy through the spinal column to join the male energy located at the center of the head. This union is called yoga.

This is inherent in the nature of Vajrayana practice.

III

SACRED ELEMENTS OF NATURE

Elements of nature sacred to Hindus were also adopted and assimilated in Buddhism with some slight changes in their significance as symbols, attributes, or as ritual objects of worship.

There were of course quite a few entirely new forms of symbols, which nevertheless had their origin in concept and purpose or meaning in Hinduism.

Chaitya

The chaitya is a stupa, a religious structure exclusively Buddhist. It was originally small, a repository of the ashes of holy monks, and thus a monument to the departed monk.

It evolved into an object of worship, and became larger and higher, with a square base topped by a mandala — a round one — with steps to the upper level, each step representing a heaven. The apex or peak is a conical piece that stands for the mythical mountain of Mt. Sumeru, the center of the world, where a Bodhisattva could find himself in sunya — void. The stupa represents the Buddhist universe; it is also a Buddhist sanctuary.

Sometimes around the wall of the mandala , but often on the four sides of the square base, are the figures of the Dhyani Buddhas: Akshobya, Ratna Sambhav, Amitabha, and Amoghasiddhi. The fifth dhyani Buddha is Vairochana, who is at times found in the center, or in the east side along with Akshobhya.

In Tibetan the stupa is called a chorten and has the same significance as a symbol.

Daiji

Originally Chinese, it is called Yin-Yang, which represents the female and male or the negative and positive energy. The union symbolizes a balanced proportion of the yin (negative) and the yang (positive) forces in nature.

The dots in each nucleus stand for the permutation in life: with the white dot expanding to entirely remove the darkness or the shadow in life, and with the black dot expanding to eventually remove the bright side of life.

In Buddhism it is called Daiji, which represents the cycle of rebirth — samsara — and Nirvana, the state of peace.

In Tibetan Buddhism it is called Yub-yam. In Tantra it represents the yuganaddha position: the sexual embrace or total union of opposites, the male and female, or of wisdom and creative energy.

CHANDRA

Whether it is in the shape of a new or full moon, it symbolizes the complementariness of opposites; also altruistic aspirations to attain Buddhahood for the sake of others; and represents the desire to acquire a method or a spiritual path and follow it.

In Buddhism it is often depicted above the images of deities.

SURYA

Among Hindus it stands for the sun god. Among Buddhists, as a ritual sign in association with the moon, it represents the unity between relative and absolute truth. It symbolizes the ultimate wisdom of a Bodhisattva, the recognition of nothingness, and the true mode of existence. It usually appears on the upper part of a thangka painting. It is an attribute of Akashgarbha.

Six-Pointed Star

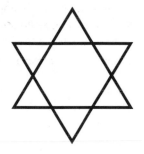

The six-pointed star in Buddhism has the same significance as in Hinduism: it represents the union of the female and male principles. Among the Buddhists it is also used in preparing an astrological chart.

Swastika

In Buddhism it is one of the sixty-five marks of Buddhahood, usually located in the sole of the foot. It also represents the esoteric doctrine of the Buddha.

In Tibetan Buddhism it is called Yung-Drung, but the swastika that spins outward is called Nango or outer door. The one that goes anti-clockwise is called the inner door or Tzhigo. The former is an auspicious sign; the latter is inauspicious.

AGNI

Originally in ancient times it was used as a war weapon. Both among the Hindus and the Buddhists, it is a sacrificial offering, or makes up the main element in a sacrificial ritual.

CHAKRA

In Buddhism it symbolizes the Wheel of the Law, which turns twelve times on three revolutions for each four Noble Truths. It is represented with eight spokes, which stand for the Eightfold Paths of salvation.

In Tibetan this is known as Khor-lo.

Dharmachakra

This dharmachakra stands also for the Wheel of the Law, but it signifies completion and salvation attained through the Buddha's teachings.

It therefore represents the teachings of the Buddha. It is transmitted from the Buddha to his disciples, and from teachers to bhikus or monks, who are instructed on how to prepare to receive the Dharma. The Dharma is not just given to anyone who is ignorant and not ready to receive it. The giving and the acceptance is the wheeling motion of the Dharma — The Law.

Mayurapiccha

This is the peacock that thrives in a poisonous environment and produces lustre in its feathers.

Among Hindus it is an attribute of Hindu deities like Krishna.

In Buddhism it is a symbol of being immune from all kinds of poisons, and from worldly temptations.

PADMA

The lotus, which grows in muddy swamps, symbolizes the purity of the Boddhisattva, who rises above the bonds of cyclic existence, uncontaminated by the confusion of the world. It represents discriminating wisdom and penetrating insight into emptiness or the void.

It is the pedestal of the Lord Buddha. It is where the scriptures of the Perfect Wisdom — the Dharma — symbolically rest, along with the flaming sword of total awareness that severs the root of ignorance.

NILOTPALA

This is the open lotus flower regarded as the Day or White Lotus. As a symbol it could be any color except blue, which is the color of the Night Lotus. It symbolizes purity of descent.

It is an attribute of Manjushree and the Green Tara, the consort of the Dhyani Buddha. It is an ornament of Avalokiteswar and Padmapani, the 'all-observing lord with the lotus in his hand.'

Utpala

This is the half-open lotus flower, which stands for the Night Lotus. Its color is blue and symbolizes the self-created — Swayambhu — and the female principle in the Vajrayana tradition.

Pink Lotus

In Tibetan Buddhism the pink lotus flower is a solar symbol.

NAGA

Among Hindus the naga is worshipped as a deity.

In Buddhism it is the guardian of the Buddhist Dharma. The dharma was given by the Buddha to all the nagas to guard until mankind had become wise enough to know the truth.

It is also believed to be the protector of the Buddha as a reincarnation of Vishnu.

NAKULA

Among the Hindus it is the Keeper of all jewels or wealth for the deity Kubera, the god of wealth. Among the Buddhists it has the same significance, except that the name of the Nakula is Jambala.

MRIGA

The antelope symbolizes kindness and consideration for others; it also represents enlightened motives and the cultivation of a kind and compassionate attitude towards others.

Shopping List

IV

SACRED Weapons

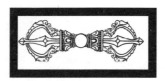

The divine weapons in the Hindu pantheon were also taken up and adopted by Buddhism.

Structurally and in form they remained unchanged, except for their purpose or significance as symbols, attributes or ritual artefacts in worship, to suit the new creed.

VAJRAKILA

This is a scepter used in ritual slaying — it is used to kill an enemy by using it on his effigy. It is regarded as possessing magic power.

In Tibetan it is called phurbu, an essential ritual artefact to the sacred mask-dance. It is regarded as a powerful weapon that keeps diseases and evil spirits at bay and combats the enemies of The Law. It controls demonic forces, nails them down and places them under the power of the Doctrine or Dharma.

It symbolizes the penetration or breaking through of insight.

In ritual worship along with the bell, the thunderbolt scepter is regarded as a token of stability of method.

The holder of a vajra scepter is known as the 'Dorje -Tzang'.

PARASHU

This is a battle-axe, a heavy weapon for cutting or chopping. As a ritual object it stands for the power to sever all worldly ties or attachments.

Kartika

This is a knife, a sharp blade with a vajra as handle. As a ritual artefact it symbolizes disintegration of all matter, also the severance of all worldly bonds, and their transformation into positive forces.

In Tibetan this is a ritual instrument for cutting up corpses, in what is known as 'sky burial' to feed the vultures in the mountains.

Trishul

This trident among Hindus is the symbol of Shiva. Among Buddhists it is known as the Tri Ratna, the threefold jewel: the Buddha, the Dharma, and the Sangha: the Lord Buddha, the Dharma or The Law, and the Community of monks.

GHANTA

The bell originally stood for instability, for something transient, and later represented the female principle, which symbolizes wisdom and purpose.

The ghanta illustrated here has a vajra handle — this is a symbol for 'path and purpose' in union here which leads to enlightenment.

With the thunderbolt scepter, in Tibetan ritual worship the bell is held in the left hand, which represents wisdom or impermanence.

KHETAKA

This is a battle shield, employed to ward off the blows of the enemy. It later became a ritual artefact and came to symbolize the Dharma as the protector from evil.

Vajra

This thunderbolt originally was the symbol of the Vedic god Indra: it represents lightning.

Among the Buddhists it is the symbol of the imperturbable male principle, which stands for the upaya or method or path. There are five points that symbolize the five jivas or conquerors — the five Dhyani Buddhas.

In Tibetan the vajra is known as the Dorje, a tantric symbol for the absolute, beyond all opposites, and represents the three jewels, and also the union of the spiritual and the material world. Among the Tibetans it is also a symbol of unity and strength.

Visvavajra

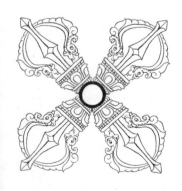

This is a double thunderbolt. It symbolizes the conclusion of all actions; it also represents the Absolute as being everywhere, omnipresent.

In Tibetan it stands for the Wheel of the Good Law; it is indestructible.

In Tantra it designates sunya — void — which cannot be cut or destroyed, but which destroys all evil. It is the emblem of Amaghasiddhi.

KHADGA

This is a ritual 'flaming sword' which symbolizes the destroyer of all ignorance, and is regarded as representing enlightenment. It is also called Prajna Khaga or the sword of wisdom, and has luminous rays issuing out of it, which destroy ignorance.

It is a special symbol of Manjushree.

GADA

This is a club; a war weapon employed in close combat. As a ritual object it stands for the symbol of office.

CHAPA-SHARA

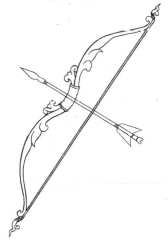

The shara, or arrow, is the symbol of alertness and consciousness. Like the sword and spear, it symbolizes the ultimate Boddhicitta, which severs the roots of cyclic existence.

The chapa, or bow, in combination with the arrow, symbolizes purpose, method or path and wisdom; also firm and accurate determination.

DANDA

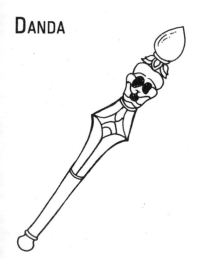

This is usually a stick or a baton, but is regarded here as a scepter. As a ritual artefact it is made of human bone decorated with a skull and a ratna, which is placed there as a knob. It symbolizes dominance.

KHATVANGA

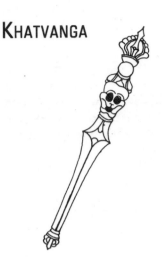

This staff is not an ordinary one. It is ornately decorated with a skull and a vajra on top of it. It is regarded as possessing magical powers, and hence, is the symbol of supernatural power – siddhi.

ANKUSHA

In its ordinary form it is actually a goad with a hook used as an elephant's prod. As a ritual artefact it symbolizes the hook which can lift anyone from his doubts or the Doctrine of the Buddha.

V

RITUAL ARTEFACTS

Hindu ritual artefacts adopted by Buddhism remained unchanged even in their original purpose and significance, with the symbols, however, ascribed now to the Buddha or emerging Boddhisattvas as attributes.

There are quite a few ritual artefacts developed and introduced by Tibetan lamas, which are unique in their inspiration.

DHAR-DJUK

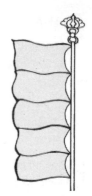

This is the Tibetan prayer flag. Like the prayer wheel (mane), it is an indigenous concept and distinctly identifies Tibetan establishments.

It is made up of five colors: blue (nan-ngun) at the top end representing the sky; white (tinka-davos) for the clouds; red (farhmath) for the atmosphere; yellow (shazu) for the sun and green (tshu-jhang) for the earth. These colors are interchangeable in position and there can be more emphasis on one or two colors. These colors are also associated with the five dhyani Buddhas.

The prayers (parshing) are actually etched on wooden planks, then inked with the cloth pressed on them to print the prayers. The cloth is usually hung on a flagpole, but could also be hung horizontally on a rooftop and often shrouded with a white shawl called katakhi, — important for marriages rituals and the dead.

Prayer flags are replaced annually during the Tibetan New Year in February. There are also different banners for deities and other purposes.

PRANAM

This is a symbol of spiritualism. It is an obeisance, but at the same time is used as a greeting.

On meeting a friend one says, "Namaskar" or "Namaste."

In Tibetan they say "Tashi Delek" which means "I wish you well."

MONK'S ROBES

The Mahayana monk's robe is usually saffron in color. It symbolizes the Sangha, the community of monks, but represents renunciation of worldly life.

The Tibetan monks, on the other hand, have a yellow and maroon colored robe, also signifying renunciation of worldly life in pursuit of the attainment of Buddhahood.

Members of the sangha live in monasteries: in Tibetan they are called gompas. They are unlike the Sadhus of India, but they similarly live by begging.

AKSHAMALA

The akshamala is a string of 108 beads. The mantra is articulated loudly or mentally over each bead. Two akshamalas joined together serve as a way of counting the rounds made.

In the Buddhist tradition this is a special attribute of Avalokiteswar, who has an akshamala made of crystal beads. When it is turned it means he is drawing the people out of cyclic existence and leading them to Nirvana.

MANE

This is a large prayer-wheel, usually a row of eight or more of these large mane are placed at entrances of temples and are turned by worshippers going into the temple. Some are very large, the size of a room and are rather heavy to turn. The mane is turned clockwise on entering the sacred precincts of temples.

Mane Laro

This is a hand prayer wheel and is exclusively of Tibetan origin. The mantra Om Mane Padme Hum is inscribed on the outer wall of the wheel. Inside the wheel is a scroll in which the mantra is written many times. It is also whirled clockwise. Apparently the mantra is activated each time the wheel is rotated.

Like the Tibetan prayer flag, the prayer wheel is exclusively Tibetan.

Prasad

Ritual sacrifice or ritual offering is universal. In Buddhism it has changed greatly from the Hindu practice; food, mainly fruits, are offered for the Divine to bless. It also acknowledges divine munificence in the abundance of the offering.

In Tibetan this is known as Torma — food for the gods. Only after the prayers have been said does the food offering become prasad. Some of it is given to the people and animals, even ghosts or unseen spirits, but most of it goes to the lamas or monks.

DAMARU

Among the Hindus this is an attribute of Shiva as Nataraj, the Dancing Shiva. Apparently he dances only when he is angry. Among the Buddhists it serves as a ritual rattle.

SANKHA

In Vedic times this used to be a trumpet to announce the start of battle. In Buddhism it is used to announce the glory of the holy name. The Tibetan conch shell has a metal mouthpiece.

KANGLING

This is a ritual trumpet made of human thighbone. When blown it serves to drive away evil spirits. It is used by Tibetan lamas.

Khakkara

This is a rattle attached to the top end of a staff. It is used by monks to announce their arrival or presence.

VI

PARAPHERNALIA OF WORSHIP

Except for a few, most of the ritual paraphernalia used in Buddhism has been borrowed from Hinduism. In form and meaning they remain basically the same, except that they have been transformed in significance or purpose to ascribe them to Buddhist philosophy or principles, or the Buddha and the Bodhisattvas.

Vanaspati

This is the mask. It is pre-Vedic. It is called vanaspati, a personification of the divine presence. It displays the illusion but hides the real.

It is also pre-Buddhist. Apparently there had been widespread worship of the devil or fire, which must have found its way to Tibet. In Tibet Bon-po, the worship of the demon was prevalent until the introduction of Buddhism. The mask here represents both the good and bad sides of a deity. Among the Tibetans the fire ritual represents purification.

The kirtimukha is a mystic mask that means the 'Face of Glory' but it has generally grotesque aspects, ferocious and terrifying. It is diabolical and is meant to frighten the devil himself. The fierce deities are regarded as the guardians of the Buddha.

Adarsha

This is a mirror. As a ritual artefact it symbolizes emptiness or lack of substance in the phenomenal world.

Thangkas

These are uniquely Tibetan. They are almost like mandalas, conceived and prepared in the same manner, but they are paintings also invested with the spirit of a deity to whom they are consecrated. There are numerous thangkas as there are Buddhas and Boddhisattvas in the Buddhist pantheon. The deity is usually painted in the middle.

They are also ritual artefacts, worshipped like icons. Unlike icons, they are light and therefore can be carried around by the devotee.

Khata

This is a Tibetan white sacred scarf, usually four yards long and one yard wide, a symbol of welcome or of offering. When offered but given back, it becomes a talisman, a token of protection.

It is given to one going on a long journey for his safe return. It is usually draped around portraits of the Buddha or the Dalai Lama, and on prayer-flags.

MUKHA

This is a ritual crown worn by a Buddhist priest of the vajrayana discipline during a religious rite. The crown is invariably adorned by four or five dhyani Buddhas, which established the cosmic principle.

It is adorned by a vajra at the top, which symbolizes the fifth member – Amoghrasiddhi.

GAU

This is a tiny altar with a small figurine of the owner's deity – Ishtadevata – wrapped in silk. On a journey it is usually carried by the owner.

It is made of two parts to form a box; the façade, which is decorated, has an opening through which the deity can be seen.

CHAMARA

This is a fly-whisk. Usually it is made from the end section of a yak's tail. It is a sign of dignity.

PASHA

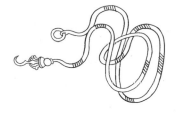

The pasha is a rope or a noose. As a ritual object, its purpose is the trapping or ensnaring of demons; it also represents the power to lift up those who have strayed from the Dharma – The Law.

PUSTAKA

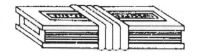

The pustaka is a book, which contains the text on the 'Perfect Insight', the Prajnaparamita. It is the symbol of transcendental wisdom, of learning and the arts, and is supposed to have been entrusted to the Nagas to guard and protect mankind until they have acquired enough wisdom to be able to accept the Dharma. It is often depicted resting on a lotus.

RATNA MANI

This is a jewel, an oval stone. As ritual paraphernalia it stands for the 'Jewel of the Doctrine'. If it is small but with an incubus it is regarded as a magic stone, Cintamani, the wish-fulfilling jewel.

Tri Ratna

This represents the three jewels of Buddhism: the Buddha, the Dharma, and the Sangha. It also symbolizes the sanctuary where one can take refuge from the world. It also signifies the 'Enlightened' or the 'Awakened'.

Pattra

Ordinarily it is a begging bowl of wandering monks. As a ritual object or sign, a seated monk holding a bowl on his lap signifies his high office, as head of a monastic order.

Kapalapattra

This is a bowl made of human skull. In Tantra it is used as a bowl containing either meat or blood, which is offered as a sacrifice to propitiate protective deities.

Khartwanga

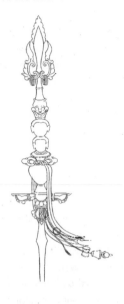

This is a magic wand made of human forearm or leg bone, but an ordinary one is made of wood or metal.

The special one made of human bone is surmounted by a vajra – thunderbolt, a skull or a trident, or all of them together. The skull is the most important symbol, which makes it magical, even without the other elements, such as the vajra or trishul.

It is an attribute of tantric deities like the dakinis and vajrayana saints, followers of the tantric – Diamond Scepter discipline.

Sukunda

This is an oil lamp with the wick dipped in the oil container. As a ritual artefact it is also used as a sacrificial lamp.

Dipa

This is actually a ritual lamp in which butter or purified ghee is used as sacrificial offering. The light itself is worshipped.

Bhumba

This is a water jug. As a ritual object it serves as a sacrificial jug. It usually has no handle but is rather richly decorated with precious stones and metal. Also known as kamandalu it is used in pouring water or nectar on the hands of a deity to whom sacrifice is offered. Nectar is the elixir of immortality and water is the source of life.

Among the Hindus and Buddhists it is regarded as an important ritual artefact and is always placed on the altar

VII

Aꜱʜᴛᴀᴍᴀɴɢᴀʟᴀꜱ

The ashtamangalas are attributes of Ashtamangaladevi, the goddess of Good Fortune. In Hinduism this is Lakshmi, the goddess of wealth.

The eight signs are usually depicted individually as wall décor, ornaments on curtains, on doors or windows. The vessel in which they are all depicted together is called Purna Kalasha.

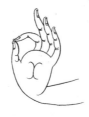

CHATTRA (TIBETAN – DUK)

This is a parasol. Like a shield, it protects against all evil. It also stands for high rank, and is usually used by Tibetan high lamas. It is the symbol of Buddhist goddesses, such as Panchanaksa and Usnasasita.

DHWAJA (TIBETAN – THANJHA)

This is a banner, a symbol of the victory of the Buddha's teachings.

SANKHA (TIBETAN – THUNGKHAR)

This is a conch shell. As a sign of good luck, it stands for the absence of all evil and as an attribute, symbolizes the glory of holy men.

SHIRIVASTA (TIBETAN – PATTA)

This is a series of endless knots. It stands for long life and eternal love.

KALASHA (TIBETAN – PHUMPA)

This is a water vessel which is full. It stands for abundance. It is considered to contain the elixir of immortality and spiritual wealth.

MATSYAYUGMA (TIBETAN - SHENN - NYA)

This is usually a pair of golden fish, a sign of salvation from suffering. It also represents fecundity.

Padma (Tibetan – Pema)

The perfect lotus stands for beauty and purity.

Dharmachakra (Tibetan - Chuyki - Korlo)

This is the Buddhist Wheel of the Law. Eight spokes represent the Eightfold path. It signifies completion and salvation through the teaching of the Dharma.

Purna Kalasha (Tibetan Tashi - Tagi)

This is a vessel with all the eight signs of good fortune. It represents fullness or abundance. As a ritual artefact it is placed on the altar for worship.

A Realization

The Buddhist doctrine propounds education, training and meditation in its search for a panacea for all human earthly suffering.

It is therefore immediately psychological and mystical, dwelling on the nature of the human mind and the human spirit. The Buddha himself took up yogic meditation to discover the ultimate truth.

The Dharma (the Law) cannot be given to anyone unprepared to receive it. In the evolution of the Buddhist creed, sacred symbols have became necessary in the teaching of abstract esoteric aspects — the principles — in human nature.

The essential symbols already extant in the cultural environment were adopted; new ones were developed and added as ritual artefacts in external worship. Eventually the symbols have to be discarded and inner worship undertaken.

The tapas (sacrifice) is individualistic. A person no longer requires symbols and teachers to guide him. He has become less dependent, now very firm with his own self-knowledge and self-discipline.

THE BUDDHA

This is the epitome of the Inner Worship where spiritual symbols of the external form of worship are no longer required. It represents man finally coming into his own: it is a realization of his own potential.

The solitary figure of the Buddha is eloquent — the ultimate sacred symbol. It represents yoga, union with the Absolute, success in his spiritual quest. It culminates in spiritual perfection, which signifies the complete cessation of sorrow, suffering and even of happiness, the total extinction of worldly experiences.

It symbolizes the ultimate sacrifice, detachment, the renunciation of worldly life, asceticism, fearlessness, the noblest state of the human soul made quiescent, calm, serene, solid and stable, balanced, unperturbed and undisturbed. This is the state of Nirvana.

In the attainment of enlightenment the soul burst forth glowing paradoxically in a state of bliss. The Buddha evokes a profound quietude, but also exudes love, a joyous, delightful state of being.

BIBLIOGRAPHY

Maury, Curt, *FOLK ORIGIN of Indian art*, Columbia University Press; Oxford of UBS Publishing Co., Calcutta, 1969;

Dharamanaksita, *The Wheel of Sharp Weapons*, Library of Tibetan Works & Archives, Dharamsala, 1976;

Kosla, G.D., *Himalayan Circuit,* Oxford University Press, London, 1956;

Jansen, Eva Rudy, *The Books of Buddhas*, Binke Kok Publications, Diever, Holland, 1990;

Lama, Dalai, *A Meditation On Compassion*, Library of Tibetan Works & Archives, Dharamsala, India, 1979;

Levenson, Claude ., *Symbols of Tibetan Buddhism*, Asouline, Paris, 1989;

Rao, Ramachandra S.K., *Sri Chakra*, Sri Satguru Publications, Delhi, 1989;

Sakya, Jnan Bahadur, *Short Description of Gods, Goddess and Ritual Objects of Buddhism and Hinduism in Nepal*, Handicraft Association of Nepal, Kathmandu, 1996;

Tucci, Guissepe, *Sacred Symbols – The Buddha*, Thames of Hudson, London